View from Bright Angel Trail: Sunday, May 11th, 10:30 a.m. to 1:30 p.m.

To the memory of
Loran Wilford, who introduced
me to the joys of landscape painting,
and to those who take the time
to walk a different path and find
a quiet spot to enjoy nature
— W. M.

GRAND CANYON

Exploring a Natural Wonder

WORDS AND PICTURES BY WENDELL MINOR

THE BLUE SKY PRESS / AN IMPRINT OF SCHOLASTIC INC. / NEW YORK

The Grand Canyon is one of the most visited national parks in the United States. More than 5 million people from all over America and more than 120 countries come to Arizona to enjoy its beauty every year. The canyon is 277 miles long, 600 feet to 18 miles wide, and in some places more than a mile deep! It has been called "a mountain range in a ditch," and it is hard to believe that the Colorado River—which runs through it—is responsible for creating this spectacular chasm carved by erosion over millions and millions of years.

The average visitor spends only 3 to 4 hours in this natural wonder, but my first trip to the Grand Canyon lasted 12 days. I wanted to explore and record my impressions of the canyon with on-the-spot sketches, as did the famous artist Thomas Moran (1837–1926) more than 120 years ago. In a time before color photography, Moran's watercolor field sketches of Yellowstone helped motivate Congress to establish it as the first national park in 1872. His sketches and large studio paintings of the Grand Canyon did much the same to inspire America to preserve it as the fifteenth national park in 1919.

In the spirit of Moran, I brought along my watercolors, sketch pads, and pencils, and found many quiet spots to observe and record nature at her best. The images in this book are now my visual diary of a very special experience at one of the world's truly remarkable places.

Early evening near Yaki Point. This is my very first watercolor sketch soon after arriving at the Grand Canyon: Thursday, May 2nd, 4:00 to 6:00 p.m.

$\mathcal{I}$ arrive at Moran Point just as the first rays of light are peeking over the horizon. I am so taken with the silence and beauty that I just watch in wonderment as the shadows quickly change, minute by minute. The sun strikes a wall of Kaibab limestone across from where I stand. I decide to capture the moment with my watercolors. I must work very fast before the light changes too much, or I will not remember the shadow patterns. It is hard to believe that the  rocks I am painting are 250 million years old.

A rush of wind whistles, just over my head. I look up, and three white-throated swifts zoom past like miniature jets in formation.

Swifts fly overhead: Thursday, May 8th, 9:30 to 11:00 a.m.

Early morning at Moran Point: Thursday, May 8th, 6:30 to 8:45 a.m.

*W*eather changes very quickly over the canyon. Within a matter of minutes, a storm can build. I watch with great anticipation as the dark clouds roll in. Suddenly a thin sliver of lightning appears to tear through the sky beyond a distant butte. Thunder echoes from one canyon wall to another, creating the most marvelous sounds. A cool breeze sweeps across the spot where I'm painting. A plateau lizard scurries over my boot, looking for a place to hide. I must hurry to finish.

Thunderhead at Navajo Point: Thursday, May 8th, 10:00 a.m. to 12:00 noon.

Toward Mather Point, rain sweeps across the canyon: Friday, May 9th, 4:00 to 6:00 p.m.

Utah juniper at the rim:
Monday, May 6th, 1:30 to 2:30 p.m.

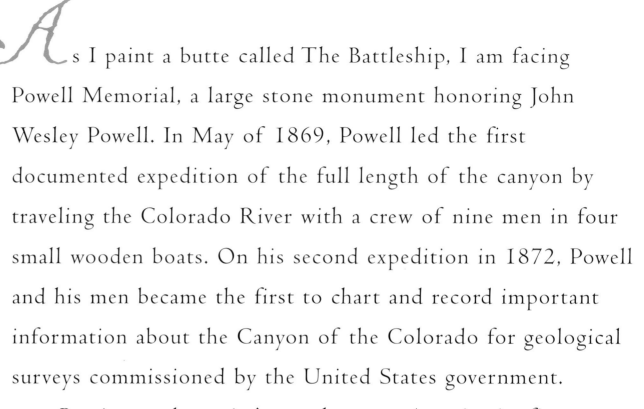

As I paint a butte called The Battleship, I am facing Powell Memorial, a large stone monument honoring John Wesley Powell. In May of 1869, Powell led the first documented expedition of the full length of the canyon by traveling the Colorado River with a crew of nine men in four small wooden boats. On his second expedition in 1872, Powell and his men became the first to chart and record important information about the Canyon of the Colorado for geological surveys commissioned by the United States government.

But it was the artist's eye that gave America its first view of the western wilderness frontier. Field sketches and paintings by artist-explorers Karl Bodmer, George Catlin, and Thomas Moran spoke to the imagination more clearly than words, and provided a preview of the beauty of the American West to the entire country through reproductions in books, magazines, and prints.

View from Powell Memorial:
Monday, May 5th, 11:00 a.m. to 12:00 noon.

The Battleship looking toward Powell Memorial: Monday, May 5th, 8:00 to 10:00 a.m.

Of the numerous wildflowers found along the edge of the canyon, I think Indian paintbrush is my favorite. The brilliant vermillion color demands attention like the waving of little red flags. It amazes me that so many bright and beautiful flowers bloom in the spring from the tiniest cracks in the rocks and parched ground. While I am painting, a large bee fly stops by to investigate. He hovers like a small helicopter at the edge of my paint water jar and takes a drink.

A curious, large bee fly: Sunday, May 11th, 5:30 to 6:15 p.m.

Indian paintbrush growing next to sagebrush along the rim of the canyon: Sunday, May 11th, 2:30 to 5:00 p.m.

I have always been fascinated by the basic shapes and forms found in nature, and the Grand Canyon offers an endless feast for the eye. Every butte, plateau, rock, tree, and shrub creates a stunning pattern of color, texture, and design. The canyon is so enormous that I must remind myself not to overlook its simple details.

Colorado piñon: Monday, May 12th, 3:00 to 4:00 p.m.

Morning at Mather Point: Saturday, May 3rd, 7:30 to 9:00 a.m.

$\mathcal{B}$right Angel Trail is busy this early morning as hikers and riders on muleback wind their way down the eight-mile trek to the river, almost 4,700 feet below the canyon rim.

I find a spot just off the path about one mile from the trail head, and I get ready for the first sketch of the day.

The wildlife is busy, too: below me, two desert bighorn ewes pass by, and just behind me, three young rock squirrels are chasing one another among the fallen boulders. All of a sudden, one pops up beside me to see what all the fuss is about. A busy morning, indeed!

A rock squirrel looks a bit surprised as I snap his photo: Sunday, May 11th, 9:30 a.m.

View from Bright Angel Trail: Sunday, May 11th, 7:30 to 10:00 a.m.

One of the most striking buttes I discover in the canyon is called Sinking Ship. I can almost imagine the captain ordering his crew to abandon his vessel, while he, honoring the tradition and folklore of the sea, goes down with his sinking ship.

As I paint, I sit beneath an ancient, twisted juniper tree, wondering how many centuries it has been here. If it could tell its life story, what a history lesson that would be!

It is believed that some 11,000 years ago, the Paleo-Indians were the first to see the canyon. Indeed, the Native Americans of this high, dry desert place have an ancient and proud heritage.

All around me, I sense the presence of the past in this timeless place.

Sinking Ship between Grandview Point and Moran Point: Saturday, May 10th, 4:00 to 6:15 p.m.

Smoke from a fire in the Kaibab National Forest drifts over the canyon, smudging and blurring the sky and distant buttes. Below, a thin sliver of the Colorado River is visible. I know that the river is some 300 feet wide, but from my vantage point it appears to be only about an inch wide.

Distances are very hard to judge in the canyon. I am astonished when I see what seems to be a tiny white dot moving below, and discover that it is a helicopter! Nearby, another flying object catches my attention. It is a beautiful butterfly with bright yellow wing tips. I reach in my canvas bag for my field guide and identify it as a mourning cloak.

This is my impression of a mourning cloak with a little help from my field guide: Tuesday, May 6th, 7:00 to 8:30 p.m.

A glimpse of the Colorado River near Navajo Point: Tuesday, May 6th, 4:30 to 6:00 p.m.

Desert View is the last point on the East Rim Drive, and one of my favorite spots to paint. Maybe it's because I have seen a Thomas Moran painting of this place, or maybe it's because the ravens seem to be more active here. They are so much fun to watch. In my opinion, ravens are the best aerobatic fliers. They roll and tumble and fly upside down. They catch the rising air currents from the canyon and reach breath-taking heights, only to fold their wings and dive like arrows to the bottom of the canyon. Ravens speak their very own language of raucous rumblings while performing their marvelous maneuvers, and they get my vote for being the clown princes of the Grand Canyon.

My snapshot of ravens racing at Desert View: Monday, May 12th, 11:00 a.m.

Comanche Point from Desert View: Monday, May 12th, 10:00 a.m. to 12:00 noon.

Before the Glen Canyon Dam was built in 1964 to supply electric power to the growing population of Arizona and the surrounding area, the Colorado River ran red with sediment (sand, mud, and debris) and washed away 400,000 tons of earth every 24 hours. Today the Colorado River appears a greenish-blue and carries only 40,000 tons past its banks daily. At Desert View the river seems to meander past like a lazy snake on a very cool morning, giving no hint of its former rage.

The Colorado River from Desert View:
Saturday, May 10th, 10:00 a.m. to 12:30 p.m.

On my way to Grandview Point at sunrise, I pass a group of young mule deer feeding on grasses along the roadside. They are so accustomed to the presence of humans that they scarcely take notice of me as I snap their photograph.

It's a crisp, clear, high-desert morning, and the sun illuminates everything with a brilliance that is inspiring. I notice a young piñon pine that has taken root on a large slab of eroded limestone. The tree glows in the morning light against the shadows of more mature trees in the background. It is a composition that I can't resist painting.

Young mule deer near Grandview Point: Tuesday, May 6th, 6:30 a.m.

A young tree grows out of a crack in the limestone at Grandview Point: Tuesday, May 6th, 8:30 to 10:30 a.m.

*B*etween Yaki and Mather Points I have sighted many different species of birds. What I wouldn't give to be a red-tailed hawk for a day—to be free to explore the canyon from a perspective that we mere humans can hardly imagine. That would be magic!

As I pack up my brushes and paints, I watch a peregrine falcon alight on a nearby cliff—a beautiful sight at the end of a beautiful day.

Red-tailed hawk: Monday, May 5th, 6:00 to 7:00 p.m.

Portrait of Lyle Butte between Yaki and Mather Points: Monday, May 5th, 3:30 to 6:00 p.m.

$\mathcal{E}$cho Butte stands majestically in the morning light. It is hard to believe that this is the last day of my first visit to the Grand Canyon, and I am painting the last watercolor sketch of my trip. Time has passed so quickly in this timeless place. As evening approaches, I visit Mather Point one more time to watch the sunset. I dash off a pencil sketch to try to capture the fading light on the distant buttes. But the sunset is so spectacular, I put my pencil down and just watch this incredible gift of nature, my good-bye gift from the Grand Canyon.

Sunset at Mather Point: Wednesday, May 14th, 7:15 p.m.

Echo Butte from Desert View: Wednesday, May 14th, 8:30 to 11:00 a.m.

View from Mojave Point: Wednesday, May 7th, 8:30 to 10:30 a.m.
First page—A juniper displays its graceful form near Hermit's Rest: Friday, May 9th, 10:00 a.m. to 12:30 p.m.
Title page—Morning at Grandview Point: Saturday, May 10th, 7:30 to 9:00 a.m.

The sketches, photographs, and paintings in this book were all made at the Grand Canyon from
May 2 through May 14, 1997, although they are not presented here in chronological order.

THE BLUE SKY PRESS

View from Bright Angel Trail: Sunday, May 11th, 10:30 a.m. to 1:30 p.m.